A is for Airstrip

A Missionary's Jungle Adventure
By Marilyn Laszlo

With Elizabeth Maddrey and Linda Perry

Second Edition

Chalfont House
Dumfries, Virginia

To the most special people in my life: my mother, Lois, and my father, Martin Laszlo.

To my sister, Shirley Killosky, who has served in Hauna Village since 1979.

To Judy Rehburg for her linguistic help in the early stages of language analysis.

To my wonderful translation team who faithfully served for 24 years.

To my home church, First Baptist of Valpariaso, Indiana, who stood with me month by month.

To all those who have faithfully supported me for more than 40 years with finances and prayers!

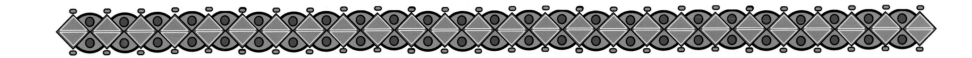

adze = wisi   ask = kau   axe = u   afternoon = naiowaka   arrow = kikid

Name all the things on this page that start with the letter 'A'. Can you point out the shed by the airstrip?

A is for Airstrip made of grass that is mowed.
By our Western standards it's barely a road!
Here's where Marilyn landed with all of her stuff.
She brought only things to help live in the rough.

aowar = bug   anasu = catfish   ano = door   apig = nettles leaf   apai = grandma   akou = roof

bathe = whau   book = yokwo   banana = yona   bat = moin   bottle = yuiukid

bee = mouu   bread = paimir   bug = aowar   bow = irim   butterfly = makwok   bird = ipiyin

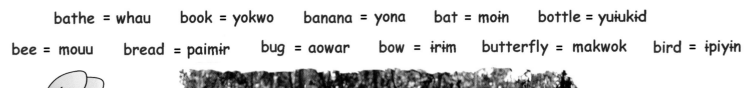

Make a list of everything you think you would need to live in Hauna Village for one week.

Paul, Marilyn, and Shirley (Marilyn's sister)

B is for Boot camp where Marilyn was taught
how to use all the medicine and equipment she brought
into the jungle as her only gear -
How important to know that God was still near!

brougwo = spinach   brouwisid = broom   bidiu = sugarcane   bombo = grasshopper   brou = palm tree

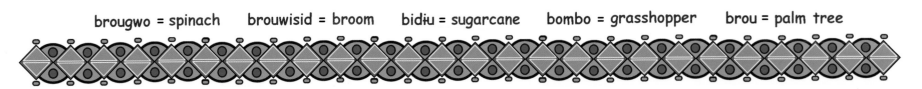

clay pot = hau   canoe = i   cassowary = hab   crocodile = it   coconut = siwab   clothes = yɨuwɨs   cooking = wɨini

Point out all the things on this page
that begin with the letter 'C'.
How many canoes can you see?
Can you point out the bicycle?

cassowary bird

C is for the Canoe in which she went upstream.
One hundred and ten miles is farther than it seems!
They tied on a motor to help them go fast
and arrived in Hauna village before the day had passed.

There is no letter C in the Sepik Iwam language.

dog = wra   door = ano   drum = iiyin   dove = inmabu   dish = mopmor

Can you guess how long it takes one man to make a dugout canoe with an adze?

drum

D is for Dugout canoe - the kind the locals use.
Men stood up and women sat, and none of them wore shoes.
They paddled out to meet Marilyn when she drifted near.
She spoke the trade language to them -
trying not to show her fear.

did = vine

Answer: It takes two weeks!

eagle = wab   eggs = y̶i̶i̶   eel = sindi̶o

Which woman is Marilyn?

E is for Evening and late into that first night -
the whole tribe gathered around a big fire's light.
Talking and pointing at the two missionaries,
trying to decide if they were men, women, or fairies.

fruit = pasnau   frog = owak   firewood = paewir   food = nae   fishing line = mai

fire = pae   fish = yipsu   fish net = hamna   fish hook = sir   fly = hura

Can you point to the log ladder?

F is for the Finger Marilyn pointed all around
at houses and trees and the sky and the ground.
Writing down the words that the natives said
and trying to keep the language straight in her head.

fish net

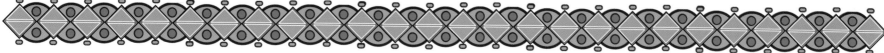

grass = ko   grasshopper = bombo   garden = numir

How many grubs can you count in the banana leaf?

Do you see the grub in Andrew's mouth?

Shirley   Andrew

G is for Grubs wrapped in a banana leaf
given to Marilyn's sister to chew with her teeth.
Natives thought that if she ate their food
she'd learn their language quickly.
She only hoped that all those bugs wouldn't make her sickly.

grais = cicada

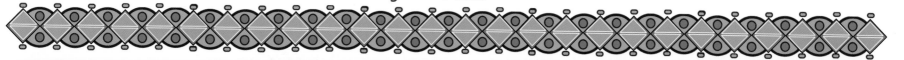

hibiscus = kɨp   hawk = wab   head = mwo   hook = sɨr   hole = no   hand = ɨina

How many children are playing?

wet season

dry season

is for the Huts they live in made of bark and logs.
They're built on stilts to keep out floods and any roaming dogs.
Sometimes if you're watching you can see the ceiling shake,
and then you simply close your eyes and hope it's not a snake!

hisrae = saw   hamsu = shrimp   ha = possum   hu = pig   hɨo = thatch   habwan = bone   hura = fly   hɨi = table   hɨd = turtle

injection = krini   insect = swapwokai

River Sepik

Papua New Guinea

What are two ways
to travel from
Indiana to Papua
New Guinea?

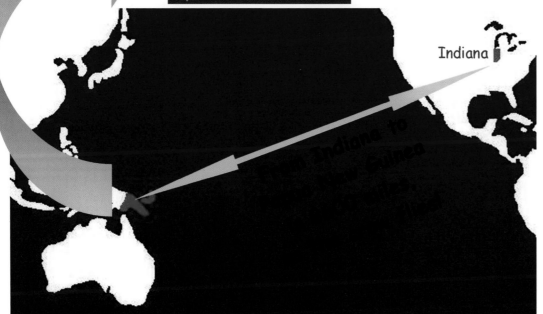

Indiana

From Indiana to
Papua New Guinea
it takes...

Answer: Ship and Airplane!

I

is for Indiana, Marilyn's home in the U. S. of A.
She grew up on a farm and it's there she learned to pray.
When she heard God call her, she left her job and brand new car
and traveled half-way around the globe. She went so very far!

ipi = stool   iwit = ran   idna = shell   i = canoe   iiyam = climbing   igwir = oar   iikam = people

jungle = nimau

How many other Bible names can you think of that start with the letter 'J'?

Jonah

Translation Team

Joseph

Joel

J is for Jonah, Joseph, and Joel,
three of fourteen village boys who followed Marilyn where she'd go.
They helped her learn new words and all took Jesus as their Master,
and six of those small boys grew up to serve the tribe as pastors.

There is no letter J in the Sepik Iwam language.

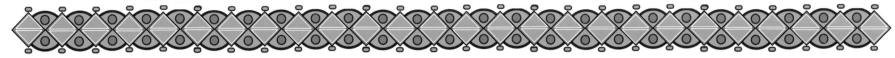

knife = wismir   kangaroo = paii

What chores are the children on this page helping with? Do you help in the same ways at home?

K is for the village Kids, both little girls and boys
who played with bows and arrows, and rowed canoes as toys.
They worked beside their parents each and every day
to learn to hunt and cook and fish in the proper way.

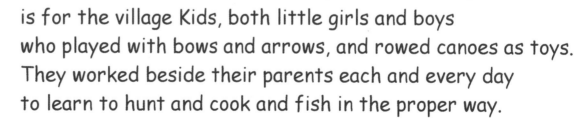

kik = wheat   kam = man   kwokwo = owl   kwaigwo = leaf   kikid = arrow

long = bripri   leaf = kwaigwo   lake = whii   loincloth = yiuwis   listen = mau

How many Bibles can you count on the table?

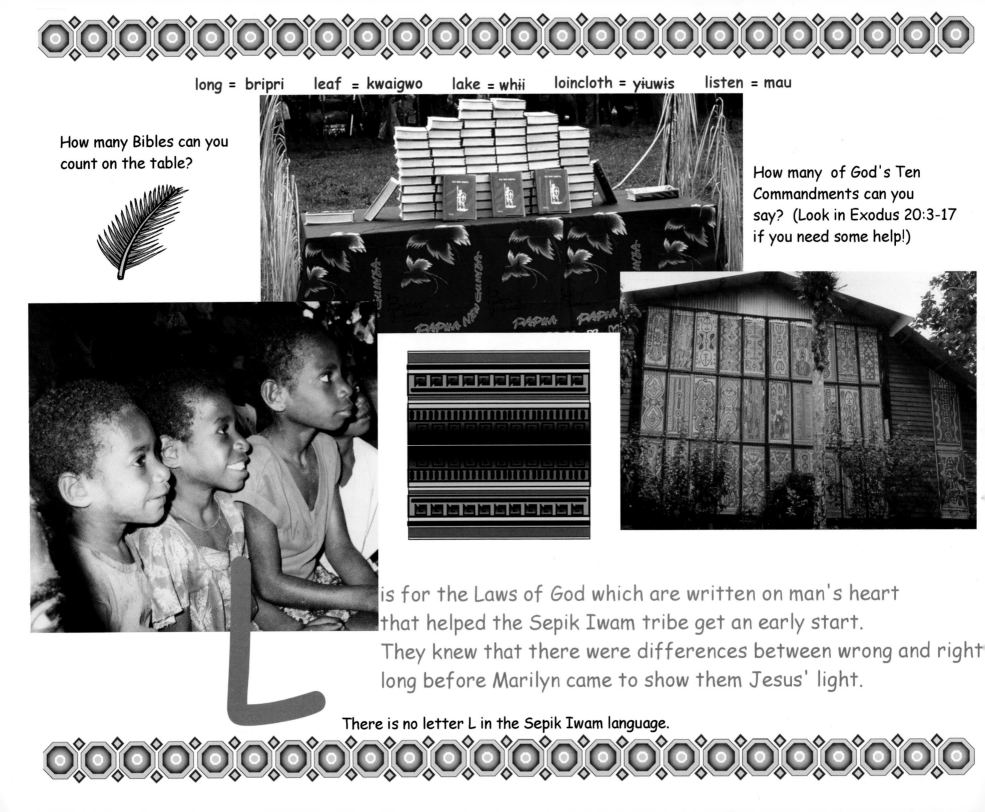

How many of God's Ten Commandments can you say? (Look in Exodus 20:3-17 if you need some help!)

is for the Laws of God which are written on man's heart
that helped the Sepik Iwam tribe get an early start.
They knew that there were differences between wrong and right
long before Marilyn came to show them Jesus' light.

There is no letter L in the Sepik Iwam language.

moon = bwan   mosquito = ig   money / shells = umir   meat = kip   man = kam   mango fruit = swapwo

How many adult men do you see in these photos?
What tools are they using?
How are the boys cooling off?
Would you like to do that?

M is for the village Men who go out every day
to cut down jungle trees and then they leave them where they lay
and wait for rain to help them float the logs home in a flood.
All that water leaves behind a thick and gooey mud.

mwo = head   mai = fishing line   mota = outboard motor   mau = listen   mouu = bee   moin = bat   mipuk = snake

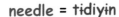

needle = tidiyin   nettles leaf = apig   net = hamna

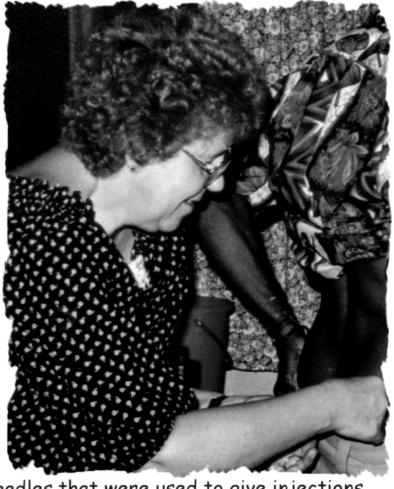

How do you feel when you must get a shot?
Can you draw any designs like those on this page?

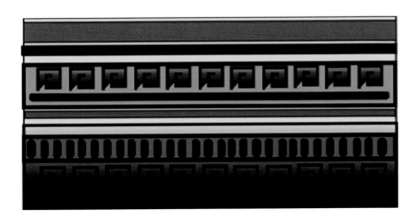

 is for the Needles that were used to give injections
to fight malaria, pneumonia, and other bad infections.
The needles often bent against the tough Sepik Iwam skin
and then they had to get new needles and begin again.

nhao = shield   nauun = star   naru = flood   nan = sago   nom = taro   numapiyin = worm   nwi = four   nae = food

outboard motor = mota   oar = igwir   ocean = yab komi   owl = kwokwo

How is your house different
from Marilyn's house?

Marilyn's house

Village houses

How is Marilyn's house the same and
different from other village houses?

O is for O-ma-ga, Marilyn's first Sepik Iwam word.
The meaning, "house," was perhaps the best thing she had heard.
Once the first word had been written, much more success was found
and she quickly started writing words for everything around.

op = water   owid = duck   owe = swimming   owak = frog   oprs = parrot   owiniyai = centipede

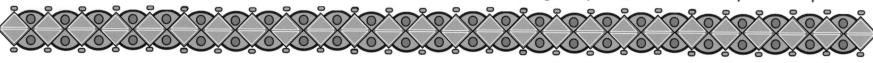

pot = yhii   parrot = opris   pencil = tidiyin   pig = hu   paddling / rowing = ki nami

cassowary

python

wild boar

Which of these animals is the most dangerous to humans?

crocodile

Most dangerous to least: Wild Boar, Crocodile, Cassowary bird, Python.

P is for the Python snakes from which they thought they'd come.
Cassowary birds, boars, and crocodiles were thought life's source by some.
It was great news to learn that Papa God created man
and that Adam and Eve were the first ones in the clan!

paemar = wood   pae = fire   piu = body   paimir = bread   pani = sewing   paekop = stick   pasnau = fruit

"See the long python? Run! Run! Run! = Ha kigi mapuk dripri kira? Dom! Dom! Dom!

What is your favorite book?

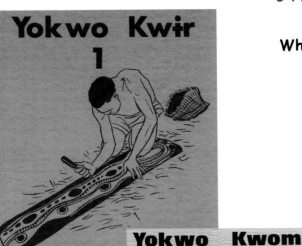

Yokwo Kwir 1

SEPIK IWAM

How old were you when you learned to read?

Yokwo Kwom 3

Sepik Iwam   Primer 3

YOKWO KWIS

PRIMER TWO

PAPUA NEW GUINEA

YOKWO KWIS SAIIR NWOKAIYIM MHOIIYAN

YAIYIM SIMA

VOWELS WITHIN A WORD, DOUBLE VOWELS, VOWELS WITH W

SEPIK IWAM

Yokwo Kwis 2

Sepik Iwam

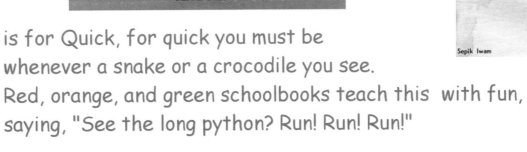

Yokwo Kwi 4

Sepik Iwam   Primer 4

is for Quick, for quick you must be
whenever a snake or a crocodile you see.
Red, orange, and green schoolbooks teach this with fun,
saying, "See the long python? Run! Run! Run!"

There is no letter Q in the Sepik Iwam language.

rowing = ki nami   rat = yaɨo   river = yab   road / path = siyɨu

What rivers can you name?
Have you ever walked on a swinging rope bridge?

R is for River Sepik with the village down both banks.
It provides them many things for which they all give thanks!
Water to drink and bathe in, and many kinds of fish to eat.
And the river helps them get around without getting blistered feet.

There are no Sepik Iwam words that begin with the letter R.
The letters R and L have the same sound in Sepik Iwam.

shovel = yao   skirt = iu   step = sip   swimming = owe   sugar cane = bidiu   spear = sau

shield = nhao   star = nauun   shrimp = hamsu   sago leaves = hio   sago = nan   shell = idna   snake = mipuk

Can you draw a face mask
like one of these?

S is for the Shells that the natives use like money.
A man must have many shells if he is to wed his honey.
The shells come from the ocean and are sewn on bark for show,
or they're used as trumpets to call the whole clan with one blow.

sou = turtle   sasae = vegetables   siiya = stone   siyiu = road / path   siwab = coconut

srib = spider   som = tickle   swae = dance   swapwo = mango fruit tree = mai   thatch = hio   taro = nom   two = kwis   turtle = sou

How many pencils do you see?

T is for Thorn, the word they use for pen.
"Banana leaf" means "paper sheets," and you "carve" words on to them.
One little misplaced letter can change the meaning of a word.
When Marilyn first said "independence," "underpants" was what they heard!

tidiyin = thorn   two = bark basket   tipnop = dipper

ukulele = ukulele   umbrella = umbrella

drum

u = axe   umir = money / shells

What musical instruments do you see?
Which costume do you like the best?

U is for Ukulele played with village drums.
Arm and leg bands make noise too when with shells they're strung.
Girls wear jungle blossoms and paint made out of flowers
when they dance around and celebrate for hours.

vine = id   vegetables = sasae

They are wearing banana leaves, bird feathers, ferns, shells, tree pulp skirts and leg bands, nuts, white clay, berry juice, and soot from the fire.

What are they wearing for decoration?
What could you use in your house or garden to make your own decorations?

V is for the Vines men wear tied around their waist.
The Western clothing sent for them was not quite to their taste.
Sometimes they add gourds and shells or a bright, wispy feather.
The lack of layers keeps them cool in the steamy jungle weather.

There is no letter V in the Sepik Iwam language.

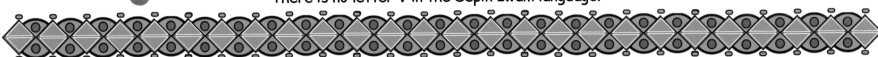

wheat = kik   woman = wik   water = op   worm = numapiyhin   wood = paemar

List the reasons you are thankful to God for the Bible in your language. Why do we need a Bible we can understand?

W

is for Wild Boar, a favorite food for feasts
along with eels and birds and fish, and other tasty beasts.
People play music and dress up on these special nights
to sing and dance together into the morning light.

wisi = adze   wab = eagle   whau = bathe   wra = dog   wismir = knife   wiini = cooking

Why do you think every one has their hands in the air?

They are excited that the Bible has finally been translated into their language after 23 years of translation work!

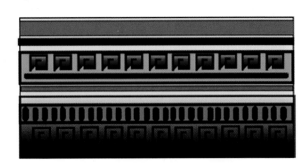

is for eXcitement echoing through the jungle land
as canoes filled up with Bibles are pulled up on the sand.
The village comes to celebrate and lets out a mighty cheer.
At last their wait is over: the Word of God is here!

There is no letter X in the Sepik Iwam language.

yams = nio

Point out the yams, the bananas, the tomatoes,
the coconuts, the squash, and the lemons.
Which of these foods do you eat?

y

is for the Yams they roast in the hot campfire.
Honey is another food of which they never tire.
Coconut milk is a cool drink to quench every thirst.
But the best of treats is sugar cane, and most would choose it first.

yaio = rat   yona = banana   yokwo = book   yii = eggs   yhii = pot   yao = shovel

Name some of your friends who you can tell "Jesus loves you!"

Who can you invite to go to church or Sunday School with you?

SEPIK QUEEN

THAT THE WORD OF THE LORD MAY SPEED ON AND TRIUMPH

That the Word of the Lord may speed on and triumph!

Z is for Zeal to spread God's Word across the river's scene.
And so the village built a boat they named the *Sepik Queen*.
They can travel on the river up or down one hundred miles
to tell other tribes of Jesus' love with songs, guitars, and smiles.

There is no letter Z in the Sepik Iwam language.